BEYOND the SCENT of SORROW

Sweta Srivastava Vikram

from the World Voices Series

Modern History Press

Beyond the Scent of Sorrow
Copyright (c) 2011 by Sweta Srivastava Vikram. All Rights Reserved
From the World Voices Series

Library of Congress Cataloging-in-Publication Data

Vikram, Sweta Srivastava, 1975-
  Beyond the scent of sorrow / by Sweta Srivastava Vikram.
    p. cm. -- (World voices series)
  ISBN 978-1-61599-097-9 (pbk. : alk. paper) -- ISBN 978-1-61599-098-6 (hardcover : alk. paper)
  1. Women's rights--Poetry. 2. Social justice--Poetry. I. Title.
  PS3622.I493B49 2011
  811'.6--dc22
                              2011018788

Distributed by Ingram Book Group, Bertram's Books (UK), Hachette Livre (France).

Published by Modern History Press
www.ModernHistoryPress.com

an Imprint of Loving Healing Press
5145 Pontiac Trail
Ann Arbor, MI 48105
www.LHPress.com
info@LHPress.com

Tollfree USA/CAN: 888-761-6268
London, England: 44-20-331-81304
FAX: 734-663-6861

Praise for the Poetry of Sweta Srivastava Vikram

"Vikram's wordsmithing is outstanding. I have read much poetry and have never seen such creativeness as that of this author. She allows her words to flow with rhythm and deepness. The wisdom that comes through her is beyond any I've seen."
—Irene Watson, *Reader Views*

"In this innovative series, Sweta Srivastava Vikram re-appropriates color. Cultures and mythologies collide along the way, and the result is a chapbook that feels like a quest. In the end, the colors are a map to identity. The child's pink tonsils or the bride's red sari are not symbols, but rather mile markers. Like Vikram's poems, they lead toward understanding."
—Erica Wright, Senior Poetry Editor, *Guernica*

"This slim chapbook is a quick bite. Poems appear and disappear in the blink of an eye, but linger in consciousness longer than you might think they would. The use of colors is fascinating to the desi mind; we, as one poem remarks, 'exist in a hue of experiences.'"
—Vidya Pradhan, Editor, *India Currents*

"This chapbook is the dazzling display of a poet who teases us with fresh imagery and delicate linguistic craftsmanship. The real joy of this collection is its potential to be read in a single sitting, multiple times, with each subsequent reading revealing new insights. For poetry virgins, this text demands no sophisticated knowledge of poetics and literary discourse. To put simply, it is an accessible piece of enjoyable writing, a concept with which a lot of poets seem to struggle."
—Orchid Tierney, Editor, *Rem Magazine*, New Zealand

"I dove into this book of poems quickly and eagerly, then slowed down to savor the words and the images, marveling over Sweta Srivastava Vikram's unique mix of grace, humor, and eloquence, which forms a medley of beauty and color."
—Susan Ortlieb, *Suko's Notebook*

"Sweta has woven such a spell with her word usage and the symbolisms that the most complex becomes the simplest of all."
—Smita Singh, *VAANI*, UK

"I'm glad I found a new South Asian author, and will be following Vikram's work closely in the future."
—Swapna Krishna

"Sweta Srivastava Vikram's Because All Is Not Lost: Verse On Grief shares her personal loss and, in return, comforts the reader. Her beautifully crafted poems take the reader on a voyage that has to be undertaken by each of us individually."
—Patricia Carragon, *Brownstone Poets*

"....there is a bit of defiance in her words as the color beige takes over in old age and she fights to remain red, youthful. Overall, Kaleidoscope: An Asian Journey of Colors is an even stronger chapbook poetry collection than Because All Is Not Lost because it deals more than with just emotion and healing. Sweta Srivastava Vikram is a gifted poet..."
—Serena, *Savvy Verse and Wit*

"This is a collection populated by a recognizable but richly diverse and dramatic cast of family characters."
—Mary-Jane Newton, *Cha: An Asian Literary Journal*

Also by Sweta Srivastava Vikram

Poetry
Because All Is Not Lost
Kaleidoscope: An Asian Journey of Colors
Whispering Woes of Ganges & Zambezi
Not All Birds Sing

Fiction
Perfectly Untraditional

Nonfiction
Mouth full: A collection of personal essays and poetry

For, *Dada,* my paternal grandfather—
without him I wouldn't have a voice.

Contents

Acknowledgements	iii
Preface	v
PART I	**1**
Eucalyptus Trees	3
It's a Man's World	4
Unholy Men	5
Poverty is a Woman	6
Something Burns a River	7
Skeletons of Women	8
Immortal Olive Tree	9
Have You Seen What Happiness Looks Like?	10
PART II	**11**
Suspicion	13
Silence	14
Scent of Sorrow	15
Ritual of the Sexes	16
Misery	17
Desolation	18
Loss	19
Escape	20
Will I Ever Be Anything More?	21
I Am Not the Shell Outside of the Pearl	22
Standing Alone Like the Eucalyptus Tree	23
About the Author	24

Acknowledgements

There are many people I want to thank for the fruition of this book.

I am indebted to award-winning Chicana/Native American poet, Lorna Dee Cervantes, for graciously reading my manuscript, and to my friend and fellow poet, Abby Adams, for her insight and forthright attitude.

I would like to thank Carolein van der Laan at the Center for Arts and Science (OBRAS), in Portugal, for her hospitality and the nurturing environment and Ludger Van Der Eerden for his patient ears and local knowledge. I'd also like to say thanks to the writers and artists in residence at OBRAS for their feedback.

I want to acknowledge my family's encouragement and the enthusiasm of all my friends. Thank you to my husband, Anudit, for understanding the real me: *pro-woman doesn't mean anti-man.*

My gratitude to Sherry Quan Lee for her brilliance and poetic vision. And finally, I thank Victor Volkman at Modern History Press for believing in my work and me. It's an incredible joy working with him.

Preface

Over the years, the issues faced by women across the globe have been brought to light. They include: trafficking, rape, female infanticide, violence, refugee status, inequality in pay, age-discrimination, and poverty. It seems women suffer significantly more than men, even when it comes to their day-to-day living. Often, women are educated but not empowered, which means they have minimal to no say in their own lives.

On a separate note, in the Alejandaro region of southwest Portugal, the centuries old eucalyptus trees are being mercilessly slaughtered and substituted with oak trees. The reason: the once protector of the forest, eucalyptus trees, are now considered worthless and problematic. The eucalyptus forests are being treated the way many women in the world are treated: cruelly and unjustly.

Beyond the Scent of Sorrow draws a comparison between nature and women. It brings to light how both women and eucalyptus trees are considered easily replaceable by the same society that once used and needed them. Throughout the book nature appears in poems, both symbolically and literally, asking questions and making statements.

PART I

"In nature, nothing is perfect and everything is perfect. Trees can be contorted, bent in weird ways, and they're still beautiful."

— Alice Walker

Eucalyptus Trees

Homeless will be the birds,
as the gatekeeper of mother
nature, the eucalyptus forest
sits on the pyre of sacrifice.

The nurturer for years,
the loyal friend of the hills
is being stabbed. Called
an arsonist, eucalyptus
replaced with oak—

the same eucalyptus trees that bled rivers
until oil grew wings and flowed with fragrance.
The flowers sang a eulogy
as the rain muted the pains—the birth of paper.

The shade from its leaves weeps for tomorrow.
The tunnel of fear
dug by the children of the woods
can't melt stained hearts.

Never expecting an *obrigada* [1] in return,
eucalyptus, like women, watch in dismay
as the world prints signatures of deceit—
announces a death sentence inscribed on her body.

---

[1] *Obrigada* means thank you in Portuguese.

It's a Man's World

It was all going well until wells started flooding—
mouths filled with cactus and daffodils

of approvals and bonuses.
A symbol for the arrival of the Bee-eater.

The slender, charming migrant
with his swallow-like demeanor, hunting

for the hidden treasures twice a year.
Hiding behind corporate sandy banks

in colonies of Armani,
singing a sad melody, attracting worker bees and wasps

to give their friends honey, then walk on burning coals.
A trap before he shoots bullets

of resentment and sucks dry the droplets of air
leaving jellyfish and poisonous turtles

for every feminine jaw and lip flying
towards success with a ring on her finger.

Unholy Men

Like the cork oak
selectively stripped of their bark
every ten years of their lives
to quench a lover's thirst
for wine in Evoramonte, Portugal,
I am undressed
night after night
until my wounds mock
the myth of one thousand years—
God was seen residing in me once,
just like the tree.
With time, death listens
to the voices of unholy men sitting
on the tip of tongues
satiating desires.

Poverty is a Woman

Autumn doesn't wear
as many hats of green and amber as I do.

Clearing the fog every morning,
I pick up leaves shed by seeds of lethargy.

Like a sailor cutting through oceans of boats,
I drink responsibilities, avoiding disguised salt on waves.

Ladles of wind spare a moment
so seagulls can spit on my hands,

a sign for the barrenness of my pocket.
Gender bias swallows my money,

I look like a starving ghost living
inside the house of humiliation with no lamps or fire.

Something Burns a River

White shirts dressing spirits,
like mud over grass in a monsoon,
while blue skirts hug ambition
tight like the night holds the moon.

A cliché it may be, but I work
like a dog with panting breath and drowsy brows—
devotion impartial
to old-tattered suits, casual Fridays.

But something burns a river—my silence
and your abandoned conversations with honesty
because I am a person with gentle feet
and no cigar to perk up your ego.

Skeletons of Women

My feet were ticklish
from the acorns sneaking
inside the pockets of large rocks,
scratching them like a dog's belly,
that's what I thought at first.

But I was wrong.
Woodpeckers conspiring with moths,
mimicking chained cries
of stripped branches dying their own death,
were asking me to put a period, not a comma, in my steps.

Too late, the fire moaned.
With feet sinking like a widow's hopes,
I stepped on a cask of ashes
only to find skeletons of women with no fingernails.
Hunger ate them.

Immortal Olive Tree

In the hills of Evoramonte,
olive trees shimmer every spring;
but Mother Earth's prodigal sons
not caring, exploit the night
like the bees maim butterfly,
believing the woman will hum
fertile songs, like the olive tree,
the lines on her hand
burnt by mortality.

Have You Seen What Happiness Looks Like?

Wearing a bell around its neck,
the horse neighs at the blooming of heathers.
The grass, like a fallen adversary, scoffs
at the bees singing to spring.
The Dalmatian gallops towards the sun
setting behind the hills, shying from the huts.
The zephyr wears a mask and teases
the buried bodies of beetles.

I am told these tales
as I dream of sweet breath
rocking a cradle, thinking of a grave.
Self-pity, I won't eat
but it sneaks up on me.
I tremble like a widow's veil,
frozen from seeing
the reflection of my defeated age.

The world is no present.
Happiness, a torn gift paper.

PART II

"Men are taught to apologize for their weaknesses, women for their strengths."

—Lois Wyse

Suspicion

Our homes had a common room—
a verandah where dried chilies lay naked
like the Indian summer.

Mothers, with *dupattas* over fruitless faces,
sorted the bad seed from the core with a sieve
thin as bones, but what did they know?

The halo of suspicion corroded walls,
an overflowing sewer of politics,
could not withstand the storm of the times.

Dust sat on the wings of trust
whispering tales of bleeding bricks
to deceased chili plants near temples and mosques.

Birds sang hymns to the past.
But like rocks, nothing eroded us—
we were fossils of commitment.

The fruits grew over summer,
so did the beard in her house, chants in my temple
and spittle around corners of mouths.

Train tracks crossed
friendships and grew fences—
obstacles we didn't see coming.

Years of memories,
drowned in diaries,
consumed by the blindfold of religion.

Silence

Like the arrow that makes a new home
when the bow decides, I feel displaced

answering to a name, faithfully,
like a German Shepherd prancing.

Wearing a veil over my dilemma,
the skull of questions is hidden.

What was mine? Some could argue.
To make a point bland as sand, I say,

Ask the bird that lost its nest resting in the eucalyptus tree,
Mother nature faced irony with a damp silence—

crying pigs chewing on the root,
molesting the leaves, eating eggs of ground-nesting birds.

The grass wilts and dies,
the trees become a martyr for a cause unknown.

The starless sky offers no help
as I walk through sobs and shocks.

An anonymous poet,
I search for my identity in the jungle of names.

Scent of Sorrow

I crawl under the meadow,
like a black spider on marble steps
trying to avoid the misfortune of a large foot
that could morph its frail body
into an unrecognizable pulp.

Like pieces of oak in corked wine,
my tiny bones emerge
floating in every scent of sorrow
where air is the offender
and the serpentine night is a suspect.

I survive
a stranger crazier than a rabid raccoon
only to deal with a beast at home
who debauches me like meat and cheap liquor.
Sad verses and lonely earth undress me every night.

Ritual of the Sexes

It stands upon me,
filling me inside
like the stomach of a blueberry pastry,
protruding limbs of secrets in my belly.
A syllable of it I never share.
Between lips and wind,
not many I trust.
Not even the hollow of my tears.

One morning, the liars wake up.
Cold as a stone in the ocean, they hear
my silhouette sing to the pink bud in my garden.
Whispers muffle *her* heartbeat. Blood flows,
pus from the bitter leaves grind my teeth—
empty becomes my cave.
My eyelids swell as my pregnant paunch subsides,
I never saw my daughter's face.

Misery

As I walk down the path alone
with tractor marks of blood,
misery pricks a needle through my eyes;
but, my dead heart turns oblivious
like the tribulations of a moonless sky.

I want a son,
the message written in powder
travels on the back of a camel to the land of greed
where all other flowers are called black roots
with no sense of familial duty.

Like the cows on the farm,
my womb is punched, again,
with a number tag—
we know who walks and survives
a shoreless fate.

Desolation

In a dream, she sees dead olive trees
float through the night.

Her fingers running through thin hair,
hum sounds like broken strings of a sitar,

playing the tune of desolation,
thick like fog, tasteless like aged coffee.

Anxious, she awaits the mist to awaken her,
walk away from the nightmare.

Loss

I touch my breasts,
tears sinking between my belly and his urn,
mourned by frightened shrubs.

I walk to his bedroom—
pallid are the walls without his finger-
prints dipped in buckets of red.

I sniff his clothes—scented like a head
stone on a grave. Tears flow from my eyes;
I see cemeteries in every object.

I speak of the things you snatched, to no one.
Shedding ravines of loss but pretending
it was the chopping of onions, not you, that hurt.

What can I say to a man
who eats pleas for dinner and calls me
the fungus destroying the root of our family's tree!

Dark are letters that sit on the tip of my tongue.
To climb the mountain of your dreams,
you sent my son to serve the nation, he came back as ashes.

Escape

Just yesterday, pink covered the wings of my baby,
sweet as honey her skin glowed

as Barbie slept in the fold of her arms.
But your verdict, tart like vinegar, changed

how she played
with the soft curls of her childhood.

Doctor—nurse after dinner, a ritual,
so games would give birth to reality, eventually.

But her eyelids grew fungus of dislike—
you were a dying cancer patient in her games.

Didn't you see her dead face around meals of silence?
Curtains of tears, a shroud for the bitterness she ate.

Like smoke, thank God, one day she escaped.
But loneliness lashes at my chest.

Will I Ever Be Anything More?

Me: A horse tied to a pole fighting
the wind tugging at its mane of hair.

You: A dog wagging its tail with a comb
of deceit flashing mouth and teeth.

Me: A cross bridge crushed by the wheels
of the car I thought offered a friendly ride.

You: A vulture tearing the flesh
of the squirrel that quietly played in the backyard.

As I climb into bed
to patch up what you tore,
threads of truth leave me
wondering:
will I ever be anything more
than gangrene and broken bones to you?

I Am Not the Shell Outside of the Pearl

I am not some denture
you forget in a cup of fine china.

I don't want to be the mouth of a princess
that gets kissed to remove the taste of a bad book.

I am not the shell outside a pearl
used to pick up pieces of a vagabond's mistakes.

I don't want to be a burnt flower with veins
tied to your birth and death.

Standing Alone Like the Eucalyptus Tree

Standing alone
like the eucalyptus tree
that no one wants—
black as black is the night.

The breeze strips me naked,
the sun bares me whole.
Leaves scattered on my breast
as orphans on the streets of Mumbai.

The dog runs away from my widowed glance
like adulthood from the language of gibberish.
Thorns drink blood,
frogs sleep in another town.

In my friendless hours, I implore the skies
to stop spitting meteors of apathy;
I am a myna in mourning.
Life drags—prickled with arrows of disdain.

About the Author

Sweta Srivastava Vikram is an award-winning poet, novelist, author, essayist, columnist, blogger, and educator whose musings have translated into four chapbooks of poetry, two collaborative collections of poetry, a fiction novel, and an upcoming non-fiction book of prose and poems. Her work has appeared in several anthologies, literary journals, and online publications across six countries in three continents. She is a frequent contributor to *Recovering The Self: A Journal of Hope and Healing*.

A graduate of Columbia University, Sweta reads her work across the United States, Europe, and Asia. She also teaches creative writing workshops. She has been nominated twice for the Pushcart Prize. Sweta lives in New York City with her husband.

Visit the author's website at www.swetavikram.com

Introducing the World Voices Series

This series highlights the best English-language autobiography, fiction, and poetry of diverse voices from Africa, Asia, the Caribbean, and South America.

Because All Is Not Lost: Verse on Grief
By Sweta Srivastava Vikram

Kaleidoscope: An Asian Journey with Colors.
By Sweta Srivastava Vikram

The Blue Fairy and other tales of transcendence
By Ernest Dempsey

Iraq Through a Bullet Hole: A Civilian Wikileaks
by Issam Jameel

The Road-Shaped Heart
by Nick Purdon

Beyond the Scent of Sorrow
By Sweta Srivastava Vikram

from Modern History Press
http://www.modernhistorypress.com/world-voices/